20 best
brownie recipes

Houghton Mifflin Harcourt
Boston • New York • 2013

Copyright © 2013 by General Mills, Minneapolis, Minnesota. All rights reserved.

For information about permission to reproduce selections from this book, write to Permissions, Houghton Mifflin Harcourt Publishing Company, 215 Park Avenue South, New York, New York 10003.

www.hmhco.com

Cover photo: Ultimate Turtle Brownies (page 15)

General Mills

Food Content and Relationship Marketing Director: Geoff Johnson
Food Content Marketing Manager: Susan Klobuchar
Senior Editor: Grace Wells
Kitchen Manager: Ann Stuart
Recipe Development and Testing: Betty Crocker Kitchens
Photography: General Mills Photography Studios and Image Library

Houghton Mifflin Harcourt

Publisher: Natalie Chapman
Editorial Director: Cindy Kitchel
Executive Editor: Anne Ficklen
Associate Editor: Heather Dabah
Managing Editor: Rebecca Springer
Production Editor: Kristi Hart
Cover Design: Chrissy Kurpeski
Book Design: Tai Blanche

ISBN 978-0-544-31470-2
Printed in the United States of America

The Betty Crocker Kitchens seal guarantees success in your kitchen. Every recipe has been tested in America's Most Trusted Kitchens™ to meet our high standards of reliability, easy preparation and great taste.

FIND MORE GREAT IDEAS AT
BettyCrocker.com

Dear Friends,

This new collection of colorful mini books has been put together with you in mind because we know that you love great recipes and enjoy cooking and baking but have a busy lifestyle. So every little book in the series contains just 20 recipes for you to treasure and enjoy. Plus, each book is a single subject designed in a bite-size format just for you—it's easy to use and is filled with favorite recipes from the Betty Crocker Kitchens!

All of the books are conveniently divided into short chapters so you can quickly find what you're looking for, and the beautiful photos throughout are sure to entice you into making the delicious recipes. In the series, you'll discover a fabulous array of recipes to spark your interest—from cookies, cupcakes and birthday cakes to party ideas for a variety of occasions. There's grilled foods, potluck favorites and even gluten-free recipes too.

You'll love the variety in these mini books—so pick one or choose them all for your cooking pleasure.

Enjoy and happy cooking!

Sincerely,

Betty Crocker

contents

Fabulous Frostings and Toppings
Double-Chocolate Chunk Brownies • 6
Chocolate Chip Blonde Brownies • 7
Dulce-Frosted Chipotle Brownies • 8
Cookies 'n Creme Brownies • 9
S'mores Brownies • 10
Crunchy Peanut Butter Blast Brownies • 11
Chocolate-Cashew Brownies • 12
Peanut Butter–Rocky Road Brownies • 13

Luscious Layers and Fillings
Pretzel Brownie Bars • 14
Ultimate Turtle Brownies • 15
Brownie Goody Bars • 16
Cream Cheese Swirl Brownies • 17
Pumpkin Swirl Brownies • 18
Oatmeal Brownies • 19
Ultimate Fudge Mocha Brownies • 20

Fun Brownies
Brownies on a Stick • 21
Ganache-Topped Brownie Bites • 22
Coconut-Almond Brownie Cups • 23
Heart Brownie Cupcakes • 24
Brownie Ice Cream Torte • 25

Metric Conversion Guide • 26
Recipe Testing and Calculating
   Nutrition Information • 27

Fabulous Frostings and Toppings

Double-Chocolate Chunk Brownies

Prep Time: 25 Minutes • **Start to Finish:** 2 Hours • Makes 24 brownies

Brownies

- 1 cup butter or margarine
- 1 cup granulated sugar
- 1 cup packed brown sugar
- 2 teaspoons vanilla
- 4 eggs
- 1¼ cups Gold Medal® all-purpose flour
- ¾ cup unsweetened baking cocoa
- ¼ teaspoon salt
- 1 cup semisweet chocolate chunks
- 1 cup white chocolate chips or chunks

Frosting

- 1½ cups powdered sugar
- ¼ cup unsweetened baking cocoa
- ¼ cup butter or margarine, softened
- 2 to 3 tablespoons milk
- ½ cup white chocolate chips or chunks
- 1 teaspoon vegetable oil

1 Heat oven to 350°F. Grease bottom and sides of 13 x 9-inch pan with shortening or spray with cooking spray. In 4-quart saucepan, melt 1 cup butter over medium heat; remove from heat. Mix in granulated and brown sugars, vanilla and eggs until well blended. Stir in flour, ¾ cup cocoa and the salt until well blended. Stir in 1 cup each semisweet and white chocolate chips. Spread in pan.

2 Bake 30 to 35 minutes or until set. Cool completely, about 1 hour.

3 In large bowl, beat powdered sugar, ¼ cup cocoa, ¼ cup butter and enough of the milk with electric mixer on low speed until frosting is smooth and spreadable. Spread over brownies.

4 In microwavable container, microwave ½ cup white chocolate chips and the oil uncovered on High 30 to 60 seconds, stirring once or twice, until thin enough to drizzle. Place in small resealable food-storage plastic bag; cut off tiny corner of bag. Drizzle over frosting. Cut into 6 rows by 4 rows.

1 Brownie: Calories 360; Total Fat 19g (Saturated Fat 10g, Trans Fat 0.5g); Cholesterol 60mg; Sodium 120mg; Total Carbohydrate 46g (Dietary Fiber 2g); Protein 4g **Exchanges:** ½ Starch, 2½ Other Carbohydrate, 3½ Fat **Carbohydrate Choices:** 3

Tip If you don't have the white chocolate chips or chunks, you can coarsely chop white chocolate bars instead.

Chocolate Chip Blonde Brownies

Prep Time: 15 Minutes • **Start to Finish:** 3 Hours 45 Minutes • Makes 24 brownies

2 cups Gold Medal all-purpose flour
2 teaspoons baking powder
1 teaspoon salt
2 cups packed brown sugar
2/3 cup butter or margarine, softened
2 teaspoons vanilla
2 eggs
1 bag (12 oz) semisweet chocolate chips (2 cups)

1. Heat oven to 350°F. Spray bottom only of 13 x 9-inch pan with cooking spray, or grease with butter. In small bowl, mix flour, baking powder and salt; set aside.

2. In large bowl, beat brown sugar, butter, vanilla and eggs with electric mixer on medium-high speed until blended. On low speed, beat in flour mixture until soft dough forms. Spread in pan.

3. Bake 25 to 30 minutes or until edges are golden brown. Sprinkle chocolate chips evenly over top. Cool completely, about 3 hours. Cut into 6 rows by 4 rows.

1 Brownie: Calories 240; Total Fat 10g (Saturated Fat 6g, Trans Fat 0g); Cholesterol 30mg; Sodium 190mg; Total Carbohydrate 35g (Dietary Fiber 1g); Protein 2g **Exchanges:** 1 Starch, 1½ Other Carbohydrate, 2 Fat **Carbohydrate Choices:** 2

Dulce-Frosted Chipotle Brownies

Prep Time: 20 Minutes • **Start to Finish:** 2 Hours 5 Minutes • Makes 16 brownies

Brownies

1 box (1 lb 2 oz) Betty Crocker® chocolate chunk Premium brownie mix

Water, vegetable oil and eggs called for on brownie mix box

1 teaspoon ground cinnamon

½ to ¾ teaspoon chipotle chile powder

Frosting

2 cups powdered sugar

¼ cup dulce de leche (from 13.4 oz can)

2 tablespoons butter or margarine, softened

2 tablespoons milk

1 teaspoon vanilla

1 Heat oven to 350°F (325°F for dark or nonstick pan). Grease or spray bottom only of 8-inch pan.

2 Make brownie batter as directed on box, using water, oil and eggs, adding cinnamon and chipotle powder until well blended. Spread in pan. Bake 39 to 42 minutes or until toothpick inserted 2 inches from side of pan comes out almost clean. Cool completely, about 1 hour.

3 In medium bowl, beat powdered sugar, dulce de leche, butter, milk and vanilla with electric mixer on low speed until smooth and creamy. Spread over cooled brownies.

1 Brownie: Calories 270; Total Fat 9g (Saturated Fat 3g, Trans Fat 0g); Cholesterol 20mg; Sodium 120mg; Total Carbohydrate 45g (Dietary Fiber 1g); Protein 1g **Exchanges:** ½ Starch, 2½ Other Carbohydrate, 2 Fat **Carbohydrate Choices:** 3

Tip Look for cans of dulce de leche next to sweetened condensed milk in your grocery store. Dulce de leche is similar to sweetened condensed milk, but it has been caramelized and is much thicker.

Cookies 'n Creme Brownies

Prep Time: 10 Minutes • **Start to Finish:** 1 Hour 40 Minutes • Makes 20 brownies

1 box (1 lb 2.3 oz) Betty Crocker fudge brownie mix

¼ cup water

⅔ cup vegetable oil

2 eggs

10 creme-filled chocolate sandwich cookies, crushed (1 cup)

5 creme-filled chocolate sandwich cookies, coarsely chopped (⅔ cup)

½ cup powdered sugar

2 to 4 teaspoons milk

1 Heat oven to 350°F. Grease bottom only of 13 x 9-inch pan with shortening or cooking spray.

2 In medium bowl, stir brownie mix, water, oil and eggs until well blended. Stir in crushed cookies. Spread in pan.

3 Bake 24 to 26 minutes or until toothpick inserted 1 inch from side of pan comes out almost clean. Cool completely, about 1 hour.

4 In small bowl, stir together powdered sugar and milk until smooth and thin enough to drizzle. Sprinkle brownies with chopped cookies. Drizzle powdered sugar glaze over brownies. Cut into 5 rows by 4 rows.

1 Brownie: Calories 250; Total Fat 12g (Saturated Fat 2g, Trans Fat 1g); Cholesterol 20mg; Sodium 160mg; Total Carbohydrate 35g (Dietary Fiber 1g); Protein 2g **Exchanges:** ½ Starch, 2 Other Carbohydrate, 2 Fat **Carbohydrate Choices:** 2

Tip Using a plastic knife when cutting the brownies helps prevent them from sticking to the knife.

S'mores Brownies

Prep Time: 25 Minutes • **Start to Finish:** 1 Hour 35 Minutes • Makes 16 brownies

1 box (1 lb 2.4 oz) Betty Crocker Original Supreme Premium brownie mix

Water, vegetable oil and egg called for on brownie mix box

2 cups miniature marshmallows

4 graham cracker squares, broken into small pieces

2 bars (1.55 oz each) milk chocolate candy, broken into 1-inch squares

1 Heat oven to 350°F (325°F for dark or nonstick pan). Make and bake brownies as directed on box for 8-inch pan, using water, oil and egg. After removing pan from oven, set oven control to broil.

2 Immediately sprinkle marshmallows and graham crackers over warm brownies. Broil with top 5 to 6 inches from heat 20 to 30 seconds or until marshmallows are toasted. (Watch closely; marshmallows and graham crackers will brown quickly.) Sprinkle with chocolate candy. Cool about 30 minutes. Cut into 4 rows by 4 rows.

1 Brownie: Calories 220; Total Fat 7g (Saturated Fat 2g, Trans Fat 0g); Cholesterol 15mg; Sodium 130mg; Total Carbohydrate 37g (Dietary Fiber 1g); Protein 2g **Exchanges:** ½ Starch, 2 Other Carbohydrate, 1½ Fat **Carbohydrate Choices:** 2½

Tip Don't use a glass pan to make these brownies because glass can break under the broiler.

Crunchy Peanut Butter Blast Brownies

Prep Time: 20 Minutes • **Start to Finish:** 1 Hour 50 Minutes • Makes 24 brownies

Brownies

- 1 box (1 lb 2.3 oz) Betty Crocker fudge brownie mix
- ¼ cup water
- ⅔ cup vegetable oil
- 2 eggs
- 1 cup semisweet chocolate chips (6 oz)
- 15 peanut-shaped peanut butter–filled sandwich cookies, chopped

Topping

- 1 bag (10 oz) peanut butter chips
- ¼ cup creamy peanut butter
- ½ cup chopped salted cocktail peanuts

1 Heat oven to 350°F. Grease bottom only of 13 x 9-inch pan with shortening or cooking spray.

2 In medium bowl, stir brownie mix, water, oil and eggs until well blended. Stir in chocolate chips and cookies. Spread in pan. Bake 24 to 26 minutes or until toothpick inserted 2 inches from side of pan comes out clean or almost clean. Cool 30 minutes.

3 In small microwavable bowl, microwave peanut butter chips and peanut butter uncovered on High 45 to 60 seconds, stirring every 15 seconds, until melted and smooth. Spread over cooled brownies. Sprinkle with peanuts. Cover and refrigerate 40 minutes or until topping is set. Cut into 6 rows by 4 rows.

1 Brownie: Calories 320; Total Fat 17g (Saturated Fat 4g, Trans Fat 0g); Cholesterol 20mg; Sodium 180mg; Total Carbohydrate 37g (Dietary Fiber 1g); Protein 4g **Exchanges:** 1 Starch, 1½ Other Carbohydrate, 3½ Fat **Carbohydrate Choices:** 2½

Tip For added texture, substitute crunchy peanut butter for the creamy.

Chocolate-Cashew Brownies

Prep Time: 45 Minutes • **Start to Finish:** 2 Hours 40 Minutes • Makes 24 brownies

Brownies

1 cup butter or margarine, softened

¾ cup granulated sugar

½ cup packed brown sugar

1 teaspoon vanilla

2 eggs

1¾ cups Gold Medal all-purpose flour

¾ cup unsweetened baking cocoa

1 teaspoon salt

½ teaspoon baking soda

1 cup semisweet chocolate chips (6 oz)

¾ cup miniature marshmallows

½ cup chopped cashews

Frosting

3 cups powdered sugar

¼ cup butter or margarine, softened

½ teaspoon vanilla

3 to 4 tablespoons half-and-half or milk

¼ teaspoon unsweetened baking cocoa

Additional cashews, if desired

1 Heat oven to 350°F. Spray 13 x 9-inch pan with cooking spray.

2 In large bowl, beat 1 cup butter with electric mixer on medium speed until smooth and creamy. Beat in granulated and brown sugars, 1 teaspoon vanilla and the eggs until smooth. On low speed, beat in flour, ¾ cup cocoa, the salt and baking soda until soft dough forms. Stir in chocolate chips, marshmallows and cashews. Spread in pan.

3 Bake 15 to 20 minutes or until set. Cool completely, about 1 hour.

4 In small bowl, mix all frosting ingredients except cocoa and cashews, adding enough of the half-and-half until frosting is smooth and spreadable. Spread over brownies. Sprinkle with ¼ teaspoon cocoa and additional cashews. Let stand about 30 minutes or until frosting is set. Cut into 6 rows by 4 rows.

1 Brownie: Calories 300; Total Fat 14g (Saturated Fat 8g, Trans Fat 0g); Cholesterol 40mg; Sodium 150mg; Total Carbohydrate 41g (Dietary Fiber 1g); Protein 3g **Exchanges:** 1 Starch, 1½ Other Carbohydrate, 2½ Fat **Carbohydrate Choices:** 3

Peanut Butter–Rocky Road Brownies

Prep Time: 20 Minutes • **Start to Finish:** 2 Hours 30 Minutes • Makes 24 brownies

- 1 box (1 lb 2.3 oz) Betty Crocker fudge brownie mix
- Water, vegetable oil and eggs called for on brownie mix box
- 1 jar (7 oz) marshmallow creme
- ½ cup creamy peanut butter
- 1 tablespoon milk
- 30 miniature chocolate-covered peanut butter cup candies, unwrapped, chopped
- ½ cup chopped salted peanuts
- ¼ cup semisweet chocolate chips
- ¼ teaspoon vegetable oil

1 Heat oven to 350°F. Grease bottom only of 13 x 9-inch pan with shortening or cooking spray.

2 Make and bake brownie mix as directed on box. Cool completely, about 1 hour.

3 In medium bowl, beat marshmallow creme, peanut butter and milk with electric mixer on medium speed until smooth and creamy. Spread over cooled brownies. Sprinkle with chopped peanut butter candies and peanuts.

4 In small microwavable bowl, microwave chocolate chips and ¼ teaspoon oil uncovered on High 30 to 60 seconds, stirring once, until melted. Drizzle over brownies. Let stand about 30 minutes or until chocolate is set. Cut into 6 rows by 4 rows.

1 Brownie: Calories 280; Total Fat 14g (Saturated Fat 3.5g, Trans Fat 0g); Cholesterol 20mg; Sodium 160mg; Total Carbohydrate 34g (Dietary Fiber 2g); Protein 4g **Exchanges:** 1 Starch, 1½ Other Carbohydrate, 2½ Fat **Carbohydrate Choices:** 2

Tip Cut these rich brownies into bite-size squares and serve in decorative papers.

Luscious Layers and Fillings

Pretzel Brownie Bars

Prep Time: 25 Minutes • **Start to Finish:** 1 Hour 55 Minutes • Makes 32 brownies

Crust

1½ cups crushed pretzels

¼ cup granulated sugar

½ cup butter or margarine, melted

Brownie

1 box (1 lb 2.3 oz) Betty Crocker fudge brownie mix

¼ cup water

⅔ cup vegetable oil

2 eggs

Frosting

1 cup powdered sugar

2 tablespoons butter or margarine, softened

2 squares (1 oz each) unsweetened chocolate, melted

1 teaspoon vanilla

2 to 3 tablespoons milk

½ cup crushed pretzels

1 Heat oven to 350°F. In medium bowl, mix all crust ingredients. Press in ungreased 13 x 9-inch pan. Bake 8 minutes; cool 10 minutes.

2 In medium bowl, stir all brownie ingredients until blended. Carefully spread batter over cooled crust. Bake 24 to 26 minutes or until toothpick inserted 2 inches from side of pan comes out clean or almost clean. Cool completely, about 1 hour.

3 In medium bowl, beat powdered sugar, 2 tablespoons butter, the melted chocolate and vanilla with electric mixer on low speed until combined. Beat in 1 tablespoon milk until blended. Beat in additional milk, 1 tablespoon at a time, until frosting is desired spreading consistency. Spread over cooled brownies. Sprinkle with crushed pretzels. Cut into 8 rows by 4 rows.

1 Brownie: Calories 190; Total Fat 10g (Saturated Fat 3.5g, Trans Fat 0g); Cholesterol 25mg; Sodium 135mg; Total Carbohydrate 23g (Dietary Fiber 0g); Protein 1g **Exchanges:** ½ Starch, 1 Other Carbohydrate, 2 Fat **Carbohydrate Choices:** 1½

Tip Use food processor to easily crush pretzels.

Ultimate Turtle Brownies

Prep Time: 30 Minutes • **Start to Finish:** 3 Hours 30 Minutes • Makes 24 brownies

1 box (1 lb 2.4 oz) Betty Crocker Original Supreme Premium brownie mix

Water, vegetable oil and eggs called for on brownie mix box

36 caramels, unwrapped (from 14 oz bag)

3 tablespoons whipping cream

1⅓ cups semisweet chocolate chunks (from 11.5 oz bag)

⅔ cup coarsely chopped pecans

1 Heat oven to 350°F (325°F for dark or nonstick pan). Spray bottom and sides of 9-inch square pan with baking spray with flour. Make brownie batter as directed on box. Spread half of batter in pan. Bake 18 minutes.

2 Meanwhile, in large microwavable bowl, microwave caramels and whipping cream uncovered on High 2 to 3 minutes, stirring occasionally, until smooth.

3 Pour caramel over partially baked brownies; spread to within ¼ inch of edges. Sprinkle with ⅔ cup of the chocolate chunks and ⅓ cup of the pecans. Drop remaining brownie batter by small spoonfuls onto caramel layer. Sprinkle with remaining ⅔ cup chocolate chunks and ⅓ cup pecans.

4 Bake 34 to 37 minutes longer or until center is almost set. Cool 1 hour at room temperature. Cover; refrigerate 1 hour before serving. Cut into 6 rows by 4 rows. Store covered at room temperature.

1 Brownie: Calories 250; Total Fat 10g (Saturated Fat 3.5g, Trans Fat 0g); Cholesterol 10mg; Sodium 110mg; Total Carbohydrate 36g (Dietary Fiber 1g); Protein 2g **Exchanges:** 1 Starch, 1½ Other Carbohydrate, 2 Fat **Carbohydrate Choices:** 2½

Tip You can make these bars the day ahead and store them tightly covered at room temperature.

Luscious Layers and Fillings

Brownie Goody Bars

Prep Time: 15 Minutes • **Start to Finish:** 2 Hours 55 Minutes • Makes 20 bars

- 1 box (1 lb 3.8 oz) Betty Crocker fudge brownie mix
- Water, vegetable oil and eggs called for on brownie mix box
- 1 container (1 lb) Betty Crocker Rich & Creamy or Whipped vanilla frosting
- ¾ cup salted peanuts, coarsely chopped
- 3 cups crisp rice cereal
- 1 cup creamy peanut butter
- 1 bag (12 oz) semisweet chocolate chips (2 cups)

1 Heat oven to 350°F. Grease bottom only of 13 x 9-inch pan with shortening or cooking spray. Make and bake brownie mix as directed on box for 13 x 9-inch pan. Cool completely, about 1 hour.

2 Spread brownies with frosting. Sprinkle with peanuts; refrigerate while making cereal mixture.

3 Place cereal in large bowl; set aside. In 1-quart saucepan, melt peanut butter and chocolate chips over low heat, stirring constantly. Pour over cereal in bowl, stirring until evenly coated. Spread over frosted brownies. Cool completely before cutting, about 1 hour. Cut into 5 rows by 4 rows. Store tightly covered at room temperature.

1 Bar: Calories 490; Total Fat 27g (Saturated Fat 8g, Trans Fat 2g); Cholesterol 20mg; Sodium 240mg; Total Carbohydrate 55g (Dietary Fiber 2g); Protein 7g **Exchanges:** 2 Starch, 1½ Other Carbohydrate, 5 Fat **Carbohydrate Choices:** 3½

Tip Instead of peanuts, try using chopped walnuts or pecans. Or try drizzling caramel topping over the top of the bars for an even sweeter treat!

Cream Cheese Swirl Brownies

Prep Time: 15 Minutes • **Start to Finish:** 2 Hours 25 Minutes • Makes 16 brownies

Filling
- 4 oz cream cheese, softened (from 8 oz package)
- 1 egg
- 3 tablespoons sugar
- ¼ teaspoon vanilla

Brownies
- 1 box (1 lb 2.4 oz) Betty Crocker Original Supreme Premium brownie mix
- Water, vegetable oil and egg called for on brownie mix box
- ⅓ cup semisweet chocolate chips

1. Heat oven to 350°F (325°F for dark or nonstick pan). Grease bottom only of 9-inch square pan with shortening or cooking spray. In small bowl, beat all filling ingredients with electric mixer on low speed until smooth. Set aside.

2. Make brownie batter as directed on box. Spread three-fourths of batter in pan. Spoon filling by tablespoonfuls evenly over batter. Spoon remaining batter over filling. Cut through layers with knife several times for marbled design. Sprinkle with chocolate chips.

3. Bake 40 to 44 minutes or until toothpick inserted in brownie 1 inch from edge comes out almost clean. Cool completely, about 1 hour 30 minutes. Cut into 4 rows by 4 rows. Store covered in refrigerator.

1 Brownie: Calories 220; Total Fat 9g (Saturated Fat 3g, Trans Fat 0g); Cholesterol 35mg; Sodium 135mg; Total Carbohydrate 32g (Dietary Fiber 1g); Protein 2g **Exchanges:** ½ Starch, 1½ Other Carbohydrate, 2 Fat **Carbohydrate Choices:** 2

Tip Softening cream cheese is easy. Just microwave unwrapped cream cheese in a microwavable bowl on High for 10 to 15 seconds.

Pumpkin Swirl Brownies

Prep Time: 15 Minutes • **Start to Finish:** 2 Hours 30 Minutes • Makes 16 brownies

Filling

- 1 package (3 oz) cream cheese, softened
- ½ cup canned pumpkin (not pumpkin pie mix)
- 1 egg
- 3 tablespoons sugar
- 1 teaspoon ground cinnamon
- ¼ teaspoon ground nutmeg

Brownies

- 1 box (1 lb 2 oz) Betty Crocker Ultimate Fudge brownie mix
- ¼ cup vegetable oil
- 2 tablespoons water
- 1 egg

1 Heat oven to 350°F (325°F for dark or nonstick pan). Grease bottom only of 9-inch square pan with shortening or cooking spray. In small bowl, beat all filling ingredients with electric mixer on low speed until smooth; set aside.

2 Make brownie batter as directed on box, using ¼ cup oil, 2 tablespoons water and the egg. Spread three-fourths of batter in pan. Spoon filling by tablespoonfuls evenly over batter. Spoon remaining batter over filling. Cut through layers several times with knife for marbled design.

3 Bake 40 to 45 minutes or until toothpick inserted 1 inch from side of pan comes out almost clean. Cool completely, about 1 hour. Cut into 4 rows by 4 rows. Store covered in refrigerator.

1 Brownie: Calories 210; Total Fat 8g (Saturated Fat 3g, Trans Fat 0g); Cholesterol 30mg; Sodium 140mg; Total Carbohydrate 33g (Dietary Fiber 1g); Protein 2g **Exchanges:** ½ Starch, 1½ Other Carbohydrate, 1½ Fat **Carbohydrate Choices:** 2

Tip You can freeze brownies for up to 6 months. Wrap them up individually and they'll be ready for packing in lunches.

Oatmeal Brownies

Prep Time: 25 Minutes • **Start to Finish:** 3 Hours 10 Minutes • Makes 48 brownies

Crust and Topping

2½ cups quick-cooking or old-fashioned oats

¾ cup Gold Medal all-purpose flour

¾ cup packed brown sugar

½ teaspoon baking soda

¾ cup butter or margarine, melted

Filling

4 oz unsweetened baking chocolate

⅔ cup butter or margarine

2 cups granulated sugar

1 teaspoon vanilla

4 eggs

1¼ cups Gold Medal all-purpose flour

1 teaspoon baking powder

1 teaspoon salt

1 Heat oven to 350°F. Spray 13 x 9-inch pan with cooking spray.

2 In large bowl, mix oats, ¾ cup flour, the brown sugar and baking soda. Stir in melted butter. Reserve ¾ cup oat mixture for topping. Press remaining oat mixture in pan. Bake 10 minutes. Cool 5 minutes.

3 Meanwhile, in 3-quart saucepan, heat chocolate and ⅔ cup butter over low heat, stirring occasionally, until melted; remove from heat. Stir in granulated sugar, vanilla and eggs. Stir in 1¼ cups flour, the baking powder and salt.

4 Spread filling over crust. Sprinkle with reserved oat mixture. Bake about 30 minutes longer or until center is set and oat mixture turns golden brown (do not overbake). Cool completely, about 2 hours. Cut into 8 rows by 6 rows.

1 Brownie: Calories 150; Total Fat 7g (Saturated Fat 4.5g, Trans Fat 0g); Cholesterol 30mg; Sodium 120mg; Total Carbohydrate 20g (Dietary Fiber 1g); Protein 2g **Exchanges:** 1½ Other Carbohydrate, 1½ Fat **Carbohydrate Choices:** 1

Tip Unsweetened baking chocolate is bitter in flavor and used primarily in baking.

Luscious Layers and Fillings

Ultimate Fudge Mocha Brownies

Prep Time: 20 Minutes • **Start to Finish:** 2 Hours 25 Minutes • Makes 32 brownies

Brownies

- ½ cup semisweet chocolate chips
- ½ cup butter or margarine
- 1 cup packed dark brown sugar
- 2 eggs
- 2 tablespoons coffee-flavored liqueur
- 1 teaspoon vanilla
- ¾ cup Gold Medal all-purpose flour
- 2 tablespoons unsweetened baking cocoa
- ½ teaspoon salt

Frosting

- ⅓ cup butter or margarine, softened
- 2 cups powdered sugar
- 2 tablespoons coffee-flavored liqueur

Glaze

- ½ cup whipping cream
- 1 tablespoon light corn syrup
- 1 cup semisweet chocolate chips (6 oz)

1 Heat oven to 350°F. Line 8-inch square pan with foil; spray foil with cooking spray.

2 In 3-quart saucepan, melt ½ cup chocolate chips and ½ cup butter over low heat, stirring constantly; remove from heat. Cool completely. Stir in brown sugar, eggs, 2 tablespoons liqueur and the vanilla with whisk. Stir in flour, cocoa and salt. Spread evenly in pan. Bake 20 minutes or until center is set. Cool completely.

3 In medium bowl, beat all frosting ingredients with electric mixer on medium speed until smooth and spreadable. Spread over brownies. Refrigerate at least 15 minutes. In small microwavable bowl, microwave all glaze ingredients on High 1 minute; stir. Microwave 15 seconds longer; stir until melted and smooth. Pour glaze over frosting; spread to cover. Refrigerate until set. With wet knife, cut into 8 rows by 4 rows. Store covered in refrigerator.

1 Brownie: Calories 173; Total Fat 9g (Saturated Fat 5g); Sodium 87g; Total Carbohydrate 23g (Dietary Fiber 1g); Protein 1g **Exchanges:** 1½ Other Carbohydrate, 1½ Fat **Carbohydrate Choices:** 1½

Fun Brownies

Brownies on a Stick

Prep Time: 30 Minutes • **Start to Finish:** 3 Hours 15 Minutes • Makes 15 brownie pops

1 box (1 lb 2.4 oz) Betty Crocker Original Supreme Premium brownie mix

Water, vegetable oil and egg called for on brownie mix box

15 craft sticks (flat wooden sticks with rounded ends)

⅔ cup semisweet chocolate chips (4 oz)

1½ teaspoons shortening

Assorted candy sprinkles

1 Heat oven to 350°F (325°F for dark or nonstick pan). Line 8- or 9-inch square pan with foil so foil extends about 2 inches over sides of pan. Spray foil with cooking spray. Make brownies as directed on box. Cool completely, about 1 hour.

2 Place brownies in freezer for 30 minutes. Remove brownies from pan by lifting foil; peel foil from sides of brownies. Cut into 15 rectangular bars, 5 rows by 3 rows. Gently insert craft stick into short end of each bar, peeling foil from bars. Place on cookie sheet; freeze 30 minutes.

3 In small microwavable bowl, microwave chocolate chips and shortening uncovered on High about 1 minute; stir until smooth. If necessary, microwave additional 5 seconds at a time until desired consistency. Dip top third to half of each brownie into chocolate; sprinkle with candy sprinkles. Lay flat on waxed paper or foil to dry.

1 Brownie Pop: Calories 220; Total Fat 8g (Saturated Fat 2.5g, Trans Fat 0g); Cholesterol 15mg; Sodium 115mg; Total Carbohydrate 34g (Dietary Fiber 1g); Protein 1g **Exchanges:** ½ Starch, 2 Other Carbohydrate, 1½ Fat **Carbohydrate Choices:** 2

Tip For a flavor change, substitute white baking chips for the chocolate chips.

Ganache-Topped Brownie Bites

Prep Time: 25 Minutes • **Start to Finish:** 1 Hour 40 Minutes • Makes 42 brownie bites

1 box (1 lb 2.3 oz) Betty Crocker fudge brownie mix

Water, vegetable oil and eggs called for on brownie mix box

⅔ cup whipping cream

1 cup semisweet chocolate chips (6 oz)

Fresh raspberries, if desired

1 Heat oven to 350°F. Place mini paper baking cup in each of 42 miniature muffin cups. Make brownie batter as directed on box. Divide batter evenly among muffin cups, filling each with about 1 tablespoon batter or until three-fourths full.

2 Bake 18 to 21 minutes or until toothpick inserted in edge of brownie bites comes out clean. Do not overbake. Cool 10 minutes. Remove from pan to cooling rack; cool completely, about 30 minutes. Carefully remove paper liners, if desired.

3 In 1-quart saucepan, heat whipping cream over low heat just to boiling. Remove from heat; stir in chocolate chips until melted. Let stand about 15 minutes or until mixture coats a spoon.

4 Spoon about 1 teaspoon chocolate mixture onto each brownie. Garnish with fresh raspberries.

1 Brownie Bite: Calories 100; Total Fat 4.5g (Saturated Fat 2g, Trans Fat 0g); Cholesterol 10mg; Sodium 45mg; Total Carbohydrate 13g (Dietary Fiber 0g); Protein 0g **Exchanges:** 1 Other Carbohydrate, 1 Fat **Carbohydrate Choices:** 1

Tip Simplify this recipe by baking brownies in a 13 x 9-inch pan. Top with ganache. Cut into small squares and serve in miniature paper or foil baking cups.

Coconut-Almond Brownie Cups

Prep Time: 20 Minutes • **Start to Finish:** 1 Hour 15 Minutes • Makes 24 brownie cups

½ cup butter or margarine

1 tablespoon water

½ cup sugar

½ cup semisweet chocolate chips

½ teaspoon vanilla

2 eggs

½ cup Gold Medal all-purpose flour

½ teaspoon baking powder

24 miniature milk chocolate–covered coconut-almond candy bars (from 13-oz bag), unwrapped

1 Heat oven to 350°F. Place paper baking cup in each of 24 miniature muffin cups.

2 In large microwavable bowl, microwave butter, water and sugar uncovered on High about 1 minute or until butter is melted; stir until blended. Stir in chocolate chips until melted. Stir in vanilla and eggs until well mixed. Stir in flour and baking powder. Divide batter evenly among muffin cups, filling each with about 1 heaping tablespoon batter.

3 Bake 17 to 25 minutes or until set (do not overbake).

4 Lightly press 1 candy bar on top of each brownie cup. Cool completely, about 30 minutes.

1 Brownie Cup: Calories 180; Total Fat 10g (Saturated Fat 7g, Trans Fat 0g); Cholesterol 30mg; Sodium 70mg; Total Carbohydrate 20g (Dietary Fiber 0g); Protein 2g **Exchanges:** 1 Starch, 2 Fat **Carbohydrate Choices:** 1

Heart Brownie Cupcakes

Prep Time: 30 Minutes • **Start to Finish:** 1 Hour 30 Minutes • Makes 24 cupcakes

1 box (1 lb 2.3 oz) Betty Crocker fudge brownie mix

Water, vegetable oil and eggs called for on brownie mix box (for fudge or cakelike brownies)

1 to 2 tablespoons powdered sugar

1. Heat oven to 350°F. Place paper baking cup in each of 24 regular-size muffin cups. Make brownie batter as directed on box. Divide batter evenly among muffin cups, filling each with about 2 level measuring tablespoonfuls batter.

2. Bake 18 to 22 minutes or until toothpick inserted in center comes out almost clean. Do not overbake. Cool 20 minutes. Carefully remove paper baking cups from muffins and place upside down on cooling rack. Cool completely, about 15 minutes.

3. Cut small heart out of paper. Place on bottom of cupcake. Sprinkle with powdered sugar. Carefully remove heart. Repeat with remaining cupcakes.

1 Cupcake: Calories 110; Total Fat 4g (Saturated Fat 1g, Trans Fat 0g); Cholesterol 20mg; Sodium 80mg; Total Carbohydrate 18g (Dietary Fiber 0g); Protein 1g **Exchanges:** 1 Other Carbohydrate, 1 Fat **Carbohydrate Choices:** 1

Tip Don't have enough muffin cups? Just cover and refrigerate batter in the mixing bowl while the first pan is baking. An extra minute or two for baking the second batch may be needed.

Brownie Ice Cream Torte

Prep Time: 25 Minutes • **Start to Finish:** 3 Hours 25 Minutes • Makes 16 servings

1 box (1 lb 2.3 oz) Betty Crocker fudge brownie mix

Water, vegetable oil and eggs called for on brownie mix box

½ gallon vanilla ice cream, slightly softened

2 tablespoons pastel confetti

16 red maraschino cherries with stems, drained

1 Heat oven to 350°F. Line 2 (9-inch) round cake pans with foil; grease bottoms only of foil with shortening or cooking spray.

2 Make brownie batter as directed on box. Divide batter evenly between pans. Bake 19 to 22 minutes or until toothpick inserted 2 inches from side of pan comes out almost clean. Cool completely in pans, about 1 hour. Do not remove from pans.

3 Spread slightly softened ice cream evenly over brownies. Freeze at least 2 hours or until ice cream is firm.

4 Remove desserts from pans; remove foil. Place on serving plates. Cut each dessert into 8 wedges. Decorate with candy sprinkles and cherries. Store covered in freezer.

1 Serving: Calories 370; Total Fat 15g (Saturated Fat 6g, Trans Fat 1g); Cholesterol 60mg; Sodium 200mg; Total Carbohydrate 53g (Dietary Fiber 2g); Protein 5g **Exchanges:** 1 Starch, 2½ Other Carbohydrate, 3 Fat **Carbohydrate Choices:** 3½

Tip Use your favorite flavor of ice cream or a combination of ice creams to make this frozen dessert.

Metric Conversion Guide

Volume

U.S. Units	Canadian Metric	Australian Metric
¼ teaspoon	1 mL	1 ml
½ teaspoon	2 mL	2 ml
1 teaspoon	5 mL	5 ml
1 tablespoon	15 mL	20 ml
¼ cup	50 mL	60 ml
⅓ cup	75 mL	80 ml
½ cup	125 mL	125 ml
⅔ cup	150 mL	170 ml
¾ cup	175 mL	190 ml
1 cup	250 mL	250 ml
1 quart	1 liter	1 liter
1½ quarts	1.5 liters	1.5 liters
2 quarts	2 liters	2 liters
2½ quarts	2.5 liters	2.5 liters
3 quarts	3 liters	3 liters
4 quarts	4 liters	4 liters

Weight

U.S. Units	Canadian Metric	Australian Metric
1 ounce	30 grams	30 grams
2 ounces	55 grams	60 grams
3 ounces	85 grams	90 grams
4 ounces (¼ pound)	115 grams	125 grams
8 ounces (½ pound)	225 grams	225 grams
16 ounces (1 pound)	455 grams	500 grams
1 pound	455 grams	0.5 kilogram

Note: The recipes in this cookbook have not been developed or tested using metric measures. When converting recipes to metric, some variations in quality may be noted.

Measurements

Inches	Centimeters
1	2.5
2	5.0
3	7.5
4	10.0
5	12.5
6	15.0
7	17.5
8	20.5
9	23.0
10	25.5
11	28.0
12	30.5
13	33.0

Temperatures

Fahrenheit	Celsius
32°	0°
212°	100°
250°	120°
275°	140°
300°	150°
325°	160°
350°	180°
375°	190°
400°	200°
425°	220°
450°	230°
475°	240°
500°	260°

Recipe Testing and Calculating Nutrition Information

Recipe Testing:

- Large eggs and 2% milk were used unless otherwise indicated.
- Fat-free, low-fat, low-sodium or lite products were not used unless indicated.
- No nonstick cookware and bakeware were used unless otherwise indicated. No dark-colored, black or insulated bakeware was used.
- When a pan is specified, a metal pan was used; a baking dish or pie plate means ovenproof glass was used.
- An electric hand mixer was used for mixing only when mixer speeds are specified.

Calculating Nutrition:

- The first ingredient was used wherever a choice is given, such as ⅓ cup sour cream or plain yogurt.
- The first amount was used wherever a range is given, such as 3- to 3½-pound whole chicken.
- The first serving number was used wherever a range is given, such as 4 to 6 servings.
- "If desired" ingredients were not included.
- Only the amount of a marinade or frying oil that is absorbed was included.

America's most trusted cookbook is better than ever!

- 1,100 all-new photos, including hundreds of step-by-step images
- More than 1,500 recipes, with hundreds of inspiring variations and creative "mini" recipes for easy cooking ideas
- Brand-new features
- Gorgeous new design

Get the best edition of the *Betty Crocker Cookbook* today!

www.ingramcontent.com/pod-product-compliance
Lightning Source LLC
Chambersburg PA
CBHW071418290426
44108CB00014B/1877